Going to the Pine
Four Essays on Bashō

Geoffrey Wilkinson

A CIP catalogue record for this book is available from the British Library.

ISBN 978-1-9160622-0-7

Published by Geoffrey M. Wilkinson
Franksbridge
Llandrindod Wells
Powys LD1 5SA
United Kingdom

for Susan

Contents

Acknowledgements

'*The Narrow Road to the Western Isles* — If Keats had journeyed with Bashō' was first published in *The Keats-Shelley Review* Vol. 28:1 (April 2014). Copyright © The Keats-Shelley Memorial Association. Reprinted by permission of Taylor & Francis Ltd on behalf of The Keats-Shelley Memorial Association. http://www.tandfonline.com

'Bashō's Frog, the Great Survivor' originally appeared in Vol. 41:2 (Spring/Summer 2018) of *Frogpond*, journal of the Haiku Society of America. As a courtesy, I wish to thank the editor, Michael Ketchek, for agreeing to the reprint.

'Found in Translation' first appeared online in Issue 40 of *Shamrock*, quarterly magazine of the Irish Haiku Society, and then in print in *Shamrock Haiku Journal 2012-2018* (Dublin: Irish Haiku Society, 2018). Again as a courtesy, my thanks to the editor, Anatoly Kudryavitsky.

Rejected by one philosophy journal on the grounds it was too 'Pickwickian', 'The Frog and the Basilisk' was first published in *Comparative & Continental Philosophy* Vol. 7:1 (May 2015). I reprint it by permission of Taylor & Francis Ltd. http://www.tandfonline.com

I have taken the opportunity to correct a number of typographical errors and, in one or two places, to change my own typography for consistency with my current translation style. For reasons explained in my Introduction, I have also made a small but significant change to the content of the first essay.

Introduction

> Go to the pine to learn about the pine.
> Go to the bamboo to learn about the
> bamboo. Set aside all personal
> thoughts and motives, for you will
> learn nothing if you insist on
> interpreting objects as *you* see them.

This much quoted saying, attributed to Bashō,[1] is addressed to poets and would-be poets. 'No matter how well you capture an object in words,' Bashō continues, 'unless the feeling [of the poem] comes naturally from the object, the object and your self remain two separate things, and it will not be true feeling but something of your own making.' Bashō's poetic ideal, expressed more pithily as 'object and self as one' (*butsuga ichinyo* in Japanese), is central to the first of my four essays. As I now realize, it is also a thread that connects the other three essays, all written later and on different aspects of Bashō and his poetry.

The Narrow Road to the Western Isles — If Keats had journeyed with Bashō

With hindsight, I may have overdone the suggestion that Bashō's ideal derived from Zen Buddhism in particular. It is true that Bashō studied Zen at one point in his life, and that the denial of all dualities — self and not-self, subject and object, seer and seen — is fundamental to Zen doctrine. But of course Bashō had many poetic ideals, they changed and developed over time, and there is no consensus that this one necessarily came from Zen.[2] Hence I have slightly edited my original

---

[1] As recorded in the *Akazōshi* ('Red Notebook'), part of a collection of Bashō's teachings compiled by one of his disciples, Dohō, in the first decade of the eighteenth century. My own translation here differs somewhat from that by Nobuyuki Yuasa reproduced on page 12 below.

[2] Haruo Shirane, for instance, argues that it does not derive primarily from Zen but '[has] more to do with the poet's need both to transform and to be rooted in the cultural landscape', while elsewhere he discusses *butsuga ichinyo* in terms of 'spiritual cultivation'. Haruo Shirane, *Traces of Dreams: Landscape, Cultural Memory, and the Poetry of Bashō* (Stanford: Stanford University Press, 1998), pp. 45, 261-62.

3

wording to tone down my references to Zen while acknowledging the influence of Buddhism in general, which is pervasive in Japanese literature. Whatever the origin of Bashō's ideal, however, few would dispute that he was a master practitioner of 'object and self as one' in his mature poetry, or that one of the most exquisite examples, in his travel sketch *Oku no hosomichi* (*The Narrow Road to the Deep North*), is the depiction of the beach near Tsuruga:

浪の間や小貝にまじる萩の塵

nami no ma ya
kogai ni majiru
hagi no chiri

Mingled in the waves —
little red shells and
tatters of bush clover[3]

Bashō's ideal is central to my first essay because it immediately invites comparison with John Keats's notion of 'annihilating' the self, which recurs in various guises throughout Keats's letters, and which provides a rich vocabulary for likening two poets who seem so *unalike* in other respects. One thing the comparison makes strikingly clear is that in spirit, if not in cultural and linguistic particulars, much of what Keats says could equally have been uttered by Bashō, and vice versa. As it happens, it was Keats who wrote 'A Poet [...] has no Identity — he is continually [informing?] — and filling some other Body', and who conjured up the 'other Body' as a sparrow picking about the gravel under the poet's window. Yet it is not hard to imagine Bashō invoking exactly the same image: 'Go to the sparrow to learn about the sparrow,' he would have said. Likewise, Keats might well have been speaking for Bashō when he declared that 'Poetry should be great & unobtrusive, a thing which enters into one's soul, and does not startle it or amaze it with itself but with its subject.' Keats's poetic ideal, then, is at one with

---

[3] Now nearing the end of his 1,500-mile journey around northern Japan and travelling alone (his companion, Sora, has been taken ill), Bashō has reached the beach on the Japan Sea coast made famous in a poem by the twelfth-century priest-poet Saigyō. Again with hindsight, I have amended the second line of my original translation from 'small shells and' to 'little red shells and' to recognize that Bashō is alluding to Saigyō's poem, which asks rhetorically whether the place gets its name, Ironohama (literally, 'Colour Beach'), from the tiny red shells (*masuho no kogai*) found there.

Bashō's: if the feeling does not come naturally from the object itself, it is something imposed or fabricated by the poet, not true feeling.

Through these and many other quotations (all fully referenced in my footnotes), I try to suggest that Bashō and Keats share not just some of their sensibilities and ideals, but a larger intuition into the nature of the world, our relations with it, and with each other. For Bashō, we are all travellers, yet bad travellers, too preoccupied with our own opinions, cares and ambitions to grasp the reality of the world around us: stop, he says, and take time to see the pine in the pine and the bamboo in the bamboo. For Keats, if only we could learn not to dispute or assert but to *whisper results to our neighbours*, 'Humanity instead of being a wide heath of Furse and Briars with here and there a remote Oak or Pine, would become a grand democracy of Forest Trees.' In our frenetic, unreflective, and strident age, surely we would do well to heed both Bashō and Keats.

Bashō's Frog, the Great Survivor

However much we may think we see the pine in the pine, in fact what most of us find there will be conditioned by our temperament, our interests and sympathies, education, personal experience, and a host of other factors. Consciously or unconsciously, wilfully or unwittingly, professionally or privately, there will be something between us and what we see. And then the disputing and asserting begins, because we are not seeing it directly but trying to interpret it at one or more removes, and often our interpretations will differ from everybody else's interpretations of the same thing. It is ironic that this fate has befallen Bashō's most famous haiku, the 'frog', which in itself is another fine example of 'object and self as one' — that is, object and poet as one — but which fragments when *the poem* becomes the object and encounters the many selves of all those who read or hear it.

In Japan, interpretations of the 'frog' have changed and changed again in the three centuries since Bashō's death. The eighteenth-century poet Buson, for instance, considered it qualitatively different from anything in the haiku genre that had gone before. In the late nineteenth century, the influential critic and poet Shiki objected to the unquestioning adulation of Bashō that had set in and yet he, too, singled out Bashō's 'frog' for its simplicity and directness (the poem 'has no breadth in time or space', as Shiki put it). In between and since, some have thought that the 'frog' says and means very little, and that Bashō himself would be bemused by the elaborate interpretations that have been put on it. To fragment the picture still further, others have perceived the haiku as an expression of Zen metaphysics. Prominent among them was the twentieth-century scholar D.T. Suzuki, for whom the poet, the old pond, the frog, and the sound of water as it jumps in, are all one with the great undifferentiated nothingness from which our world and we ourselves come.

In the West, such Zen interpretations of the 'frog' (and of Bashō's poetry in general) have tended to predominate, largely due to the influence of the translator and literary commentator Reginald Blyth. Himself heavily influenced by Suzuki, Blyth's monumental studies, *Haiku* (1949-52) and *A History of Haiku* (1969), sometimes seem to treat haiku and Zen interchangeably. This is familiar ground, but I hope that my second essay helps to correct the misperception that Zen interpretations of Bashō's 'frog' are principally a *Western* phenomenon that began with Blyth: on the contrary, one of the most explicitly Zen readings of the haiku is from a Japanese commentary dated 1795.

The essay ends with a paradox, or rather, two paradoxical and unanswered questions. Not only is it possible for each of us to find something different in the 'frog' haiku, we *celebrate* the fact that it is possible. 'Diversity', we call it, or 'creativity', 'freedom of expression', 'fresh perspectives', 'thinking outside the box', and a dozen other names. There are indeed as many ways of interpreting Bashō's 'frog' as there are selves to read the poem. But if, as Bashō insists, we can only grasp the truth of something by intuitively becoming one with it (or, as Keats would say, by 'annihilating self'), ultimately *none* of our interpretations are valid since they are nothing more than indirect, solipsistic, and conflicting approximations of the truth. Or might it be, as the composer Arvo Pärt once said of an audience's perceptions of his music, that *all* our interpretations are valid? And are we right to celebrate them because, in a sense that seems to contradict Bashō and Keats, they are all true?

Found in Translation

If 'Go to the pine to learn about the pine' is addressed to poets and would-be poets, it is also addressed to translators and would-be translators. I am still not sure whether my third essay, which explores some of the challenges of translating Bashō's 'cicada' haiku into English, tries its best to follow the 'pine and bamboo' injunction or, while seeming to do so, in fact ignores it altogether. Does it allow the feeling of Bashō's poem to come naturally from the object — and here the object is at least one screeching insect that breaks the silence of a mountaintop temple — or does my translator turn the poem into a more and more convoluted product of his own interests, preoccupations, and confusions?

Among the challenges any translator faces are the imprecisions and ambiguities of Japanese, a language which generally does not distinguish between singular and plural, and which cheerfully omits personal pronouns, determiners, and other clues as to who is speaking or acting. In the case of the 'cicada', the lack of singular/plural distinction is pivotal, for it forces the translator to make a choice: is it one cicada breaking the silence, or two, or two hundred? And immediately before the haiku, when Bashō describes his state of mind as he worships at the topmost shrines of the temple, are we to understand that he is also speaking for his companion, Sora? If so, how does he know that Sora's state of mind is the same? I suspect that many Japanese readers would regard such questions as *rikutsuppoi* — nit-picking, making difficulties, missing the point. Yet the truth is that in English translation, if not in Japanese, we need answers. Who or what is doing what, we want to know, and just who is feeling what? Grammar and syntax provide unexpected insights into culturally conditioned expectations.

My translator has other issues of language and interpretation to contend with, and has to make other choices that materially affect how the haiku will read in English. He tries one permutation after another, experimenting with nuance and word order, now sticking close to the Japanese, now going for a freer rendering. He arrives at a final version, final but not definitive because the preceding versions are, in their own ways, equally compelling. By attempting to settle on one version he appears to have discovered that there is *no* one version, and that all he can do is offer multiple translations of the haiku. Is that a genuine discovery, or has the translator unwittingly projected dilemma and doubt from his own past onto the job in hand?

The Frog and the Basilisk

My first three essays suggest that Bashō's injunction applies primarily to poets, translators, and their readers, which makes it an aesthetic or bookish affair. What is more, an individual affair: it is down to each one of us on our own, Bashō seems to be saying, to set aside the personal likes and dislikes, enthusiasms and blind spots, that prevent us from seeing the pine in the pine, or the bamboo in the bamboo. What, though, if Bashō, together with his fellow-traveller Keats, is addressing us *collectively* as well as individually? For Keats, we feel, 'annihilating self' is not just a matter for poets and travellers; it is one of the means by which, in time, humanity as a whole might learn not to dispute or assert but to 'whisper results' instead. In a similar way, could it be that Bashō's 'Go the pine' is an invitation to humanity to set aside its larger likes, dislikes, enthusiasms and blind spots, the better to grasp the true nature of our shared world and learn to live in it more harmoniously? I hasten to add that I have no evidence that Bashō meant his saying to be taken in such a sense. While it is safe to see 'Go to the pine' as a poetic ideal, it may be far-fetched or perverse to try and read more into it than that. And yet, I confess, I cannot resist the temptation to read more into it than that, and to bring my reading closer to home.

'Go to the pine' is synonymous with 'object and self as one', the object seen as it is and perfectly at one with the seer. In turn, 'object and self as one' is encapsulated in Bashō's 'frog' haiku, which I revisit at the start of my fourth essay. In returning to it I also return to the vexed question of how far it is influenced by, or is an expression of, Zen Buddhism. This time I come off the fence and unequivocally adopt D.T. Suzuki's interpretation of the haiku (from his book *Zen and Japanese Culture*, first published in 1938 and still in print). As I understand Suzuki, the frog, the pond, the poet, everything in the world, each vividly exists in its particularity — in its *suchness* or *just-as-it-isness*. But at the instant the frog leaps into the water, the frog, the pond, the poet, the universe itself, dissolve back into the undifferentiated nothingness from which they come. All that is, has ever been, and might ever be, is both uniquely differentiated in itself and one with the great nothingness. It is meaningless to ask who or what turns nothing into everything, for in Buddhism there is no duality of nothing and everything to begin with, and certainly no creator God or other agency to do any turning, still less to provide a reason or purpose for doing it. In short, the frog of Bashō's haiku is a metaphor not only for reality as Bashō would have us see it but also for a conception of reality — or, more prosaically, a world view — in which everything that is *just is*.

The contrast with the Judaeo-Christian tradition, and with world views which have grown out of that tradition, could hardly be more profound. The Word of God, Universal Reason, History, Progress —

these are some of the names for the divine or impersonal forces to which we have looked for reassurance that the world is as it is, and not otherwise, for some reason or purpose. Bashō's leaping frog is joined in my menagerie of metaphors by the basilisk of John Donne's Easter sermon in 1628: never doubt, Donne preached, that God's purpose reaches down even to the lowliest levels of creation. Particularly since the Enlightenment, we have tended to secularize the Word of God and seek reassurance in other forms. But the common denominator has always been the same: a collective fear of the unintelligible, that is, of the merest suspicion that there might *not* be any reason why the world is as it is. Now, in our own age, the game is up. There is no excuse for continuing to delude ourselves with wishful thinking. We know, on the robust evidence of modern cosmology and physics, that in reality everything (or the potential for everything) came into being spontaneously, discontinuously, without reason, necessity, or purpose, in a Big Bang 13.8 billion years ago. It is both a disconcerting discovery and a liberating one, because it frees us to recognize that responsibility for what happens in our world — and therefore responsibility for how well or badly humanity lives with itself — lies with us, not with some imagined creator or force. It is high time we accepted that our world, like Bashō's frog, *just is*.

The Narrow Road to the Western Isles
—If Keats had journeyed with Bashō

The Japanese poet we know by the pen name Bashō was born in 1644 in Iga Ueno, a castle town in an old province southeast of Kyōto. By an almost perfectly tidy coincidence, he died one hundred and one years before John Keats was born in London in 1795. Although to all appearances their worlds and their lives could not have been more different, their poetic sensibilities seem to have been strikingly similar. This is not an original observation: it was, for instance, at the heart of an essay by James Kirkup in *The Keats-Shelley Review* in 1996 (Vol. 10, pp. 65-75). But in what follows I try to give the observation a new twist by likening Keats and Bashō as *travellers* — travellers, that is, both in the literal and the metaphorical sense.

Bashō was born into a world turned in on itself. For much of the sixteenth century Japan had been in a state of anarchy, riven by local wars in the absence of effective centralized authority. From 1600 the country was finally reunified under the Tokugawa family, whose main concern was to ensure that there was a place for everyone and that everyone was in their place. The Tokugawa regime restored an ancient Confucian division of society that ranked the population nominally into four classes: warriors, farmers, artisans, and merchants, in that order. The regime virtually cut Japan off from the rest of the world for the next two hundred years, banning the construction of ocean-going ships and, on pain of death, prohibiting any Japanese from travelling abroad or returning if they had already left. Although in reality Japan was moving to a money economy (dominated by the merchants, not the warriors), the Tokugawa maintained the fiction that it was based on agricultural commodities, and a retainer's stipend, for example, was still paid in rice. In short, Bashō's world was feudal and largely arrested in time.

By contrast, Keats's was a world in flux. Britain, too, was at peace once Napoleon had been defeated in 1815, but it was a restless, restive peace and not a static one. The industrial revolution was under way and would lead to fundamental social change as new wealth replaced old and people flocked to the towns to work in the mills and factories. Moreover, while dire warnings against revolutionary conspiracy issued from conservative quarters, there was a ferment of radical ideas in economics, law, and political philosophy (to which, as we know from Nicholas Roe's new biography, Keats was exposed from an early age through his schooling at Clarke's Academy[1]).

As for the individual circumstances of Bashō and Keats, it is hard to imagine two lives outwardly more different. Bashō's origins were relatively humble: his father was permitted to wear a sword, a warrior privilege, but the family itself probably belonged to the farmer class. His father died in 1656. At some point (just when is uncertain, albeit most accounts now suggest that it was at about age eighteen) Bashō entered service in the household of a member of the local ruling family, apparently as a servant-cum-companion to his heir, Yoshitada, who was two years older than himself. The two young men evidently became close friends, studying poetry together under a master in Kyōto, and it is thought that Bashō was deeply affected by Yoshitada's early death in 1666. Whether or not that is so, Bashō seems to have led an unsettled life. After more than five years spent mostly in Kyōto, he left for Edo, Japan's new capital, the seat of Tokugawa power and a centre of vibrant artistic activity. Gradually he established himself as a recognized poet, supported by admirers and, as is the way in Japan, gathering around him a circle of disciples — one of whom donated the *bashō*, a banana plant, that inspired the pen name. However, judging by the imagery in some of his poems dating from the early 1680s, Bashō was troubled and ambivalent about the meaningfulness of his life in Edo. It may be significant that it was at this time he practised Zen meditation. In 1684 Bashō made the first of the journeys described in his travel sketches, and the same year saw the appearance of *Fuyu no hi* (*A Winter Day*), the first of seven major anthologies of poetry associated with him. The most famous of the travel sketches, *Oku no hosomichi* (*The Narrow Road to the Deep North*, of which more anon), came out of his third journey, which he began in 1689 after selling his house — probably a sign that he did not expect to survive, let alone return to Edo. Bashō did return more than two years later, lived as a would-be recluse in a new house that had been built for him, then set

---

[1] *John Keats. A New Life* (New Haven: Yale University Press, 2012), pp. 20-21, 32.

out on one last journey, to southern Japan as he intended; he was taken ill en route and died in Ōsaka in late 1694.[2]

The events of Keats's life are more familiar to us and it would be redundant to retell them here. Suffice to say that, despite all the differences described above, there are also numerous parallels between the two lives: quite lowly origins; early bereavements (father and brother Tom in Keats's case, father and Yoshitada in Bashō's); youthful ambition mixed with self-doubt; restlessness; melancholy verging at times on despair; spiritual and maybe psychological crisis; ill-health and death far from home.

The most extraordinary parallels are between the sensibilities of Keats and Bashō, and their ways of expressing what they feel they are trying to achieve in their writing. A much-quoted commentary attributed to Bashō (as recorded by one of his followers, Hattori Dohō) reads:

> Go to the pine if you want to learn about the pine, or
> to the bamboo if you want to learn about the bamboo.
> And in doing so, you must leave your subjective
> preoccupation with yourself. Otherwise you impose
> yourself on the object and do not learn. Your poetry
> issues of its own accord when you and the object
> have become one — when you have plunged deep
> enough into the object to see something like a hidden
> glimmering there. However well phrased your poetry
> may be, if your feeling is not natural — if the object
> and yourself are separate — then your poetry is not
> true poetry but merely your subjective counterfeit.[3]

---

[2] A fuller account of Bashō's life is included in N. Yuasa's introduction to his translation *The Narrow Road to the Deep North and Other Travel Sketches* (Harmondsworth: Penguin Classics, 1968). As you will have noticed, however, Bashō biography is not an exact science and no single account is likely to be definitive. All my quotations from Bashō's prose are from the Yuasa translation [hereafter referred to as Yuasa]. The three *haiku* translations are my own.

[3] Yuasa, p. 33. The Japanese text can be found in the *Akazōshi* 「赤冊子」 in *Kyoraishō/Sanzōshi/Tabineron* 『去来抄・三冊子・旅寝論』 (Tōkyō: Iwanami Shoten, 1993 reprint), a collection of works by Hattori Dohō and another of Bashō's disciples, Mukai Kyorai.

Forget for a moment the particularities of time, culture, and language, and this could well be Keats speaking in, say, his letter to Richard Woodhouse of 27 October 1818:

> A Poet is the most unpoetical of any thing in existence; because he has no Identity — he is continually in for [informing?] — and filling some other Body — The Sun, the Moon, the Sea and Men and Women who are creatures of impulse are poetical and have about them an unchangeable attribute — the poet has none; no identity — he is certainly the most unpoetical of all God's Creatures. [...] When I am in a room with People if I ever am free from speculating on creations of my own brain, then not myself goes home to myself: but the identity of every one in the room begins to [so] to press upon me that, I am in a very little time an[ni]hilated — not only among Men; it would be the same in a Nursery of children.[4]

Or adjust the flora and fauna and it might be from Keats's letter to John Hamilton Reynolds of 19 February 1818:

> Now it is more noble to sit like Jove that [than] to fly like Mercury — let us not therefore go hurrying about and collecting honey-bee like, buzzing here and there impatiently from a knowledge of what is to be arrived at: but let us open our leaves like a flower and be passive and receptive — budding patiently under the eye of Apollo and taking hints from evey noble insect that favors us with a visit [...][5]

Bashō surely would have agreed with Keats that 'Poetry should be great & unobtrusive, a thing which enters into one's soul, and does not startle it or amaze it with itself but with its subject', and he would have

---

[4] Pages 157-58 in the single-volume *Letters of John Keats* edited by Robert Gittings (Oxford: Oxford University Press, 1990 reprint). Except for the fragment from *Hyperion*, my Keats quotations all come from this volume [hereafter Gittings].

[5] Gittings, p. 66.

delighted at the image of Keats picking about the gravel beneath his window, perfectly at one with the sparrow.[6] But what is this paradox of the unpoetical poet, of poetry that is not poetry unless the poet is absent from it? One answer, in my opinion, is that Bashō and Keats both stand for an unconditional openness to all experience, so unconditional that it demands a complete transparency — or, Keats's word, *annihilation* — of the self. Particularly as we know that Bashō practised Zen meditation, it seems reasonable to assume that for him the self probably had a religious-metaphysical meaning rooted in Buddhism: that is, the self represents our attachments, our preoccupations, our striving, everything that traps us in a divided 'me/not-me' relation to the world, and therefore it is an obstacle not just to 'true' poetry but to our own 'true' being as part of a greater reality beyond individual identity. Now while Keats's description of finding himself 'annihilated' in the company of others is very intriguing and invites comparison with this element in Bashō, personally I do not feel qualified to make a case (as others have done[7]) that unbeknown to himself Keats was in effect a practitioner of Zen. Nevertheless, it is clear enough that Keats had his own highly developed sense of the self as an obstacle to truthful poetry and to what he conceived of as truth in general. Most obviously, he expresses this sense in his objections to 'the wordsworthian or egotistical sublime', for Keats's complaint against Wordsworth is precisely that he is an 'Egotist' whose vanity and tendency to 'brood and peacock' over his own speculations produces poetry that 'has a palpable design upon us'.[8] Yet Keats also rails against the self in its over-rationalizing, certainty-seeking, 'consequitive' aspect, which is the source of all that bee-like buzzing 'from a knowledge of what is to be arrived at' or, as he puts it elsewhere, 'irritable reaching after fact & reason'.[9] No, insists Keats, leave what is to be arrived at to look after itself; cease the

---

[6] Letters to Reynolds of 3 February 1818 and Benjamin Bailey of 22 November 1817 respectively; Gittings, pp. 61 and 38.

[7] See, for instance, Richard Benton's essay 'Keats and Zen' in the journal *Philosophy East and West*, Vol. 16, No. 1 (1966), pp. 33-47.

[8] Letters to Woodhouse of 27 October 1818 and Reynolds of 3 February 1818; Gittings, pp. 157 and 60-61.

[9] Letter to George and Tom Keats of 21, 27(?) December 1817; Gittings, p. 43. Keats's word 'consequitive' occurs in his letter to John Taylor of 30 January 1818; Gittings, p. 59.

irritable reaching and instead 'let the mind be a thoroughfare for all thoughts'. [10] Whether by coincidence or some more mysterious connection, Keats here both recalls Bashō and, I think, prefigures Seamus Heaney — especially two lines in the final poem of his collection *The Spirit Level*:

> You are neither here nor there,
> A hurry through which known and strange things pass[11]

We are deluded, Bashō, Keats, and Heaney are saying, if we suppose that truth is something we set out to discover as we pass through the world. The reality is that truth discovers itself as the world passes through us.

To what experiences, then, were Bashō and Keats so open on their journeys? What thoughts passed through the thoroughfares of their minds? The scope is very broad, ranging from the sublime at one extreme to the earthy and even the squalid at the other. For the sublime think, for instance, of Keats's description of the waterfalls at Ambleside, 'the first darting down the slate-rock like an arrow; the second spreading out like a fan — the third dashed into a mist — and the one on the other side of the rock a sort of mixture of all these.'[12] It is as if Keats is seeing turbulent water for the first time, fascinated by its different 'characters' (the same fascination that had impelled Leonardo da Vinci to make his sketches of water swirling and billowing around obstacles in a river?). Or think of how Keats conjures up for Tom the sight of Ailsa Craig, island remnant of an extinct volcano off the Ayrshire coast:

> After two or three Miles [...] we turned suddenly into
> a magnificent glen finely wooded in Parts — seven
> Miles long — with a Mountain Stream winding down
> the Midst — full of cottages in the most happy
> Situations — the sides of the Hills coverd with sheep
> — the effect of cattle lowing I never had so finely —
> At the end we had a gradual ascent and got among
> the tops of the Mountains whence In a little time I

---

[10] Letter to George and Georgiana Keats of 17-27 September 1819; Gittings, p. 326.

[11] 'Postscript', ll. 13-14; p. 70 in *The Spirit Level* (London: Faber and Faber, 1996).

[12] Letter to Tom Keats dated 25-27 June 1818; Gittings, pp. 102-03.

descried in the Sea Ailsa Rock 940 feet hight — it
was 15 Miles distant and seemed close upon us —
The effect of ailsa with the peculiar perspective of
the Sea in connection with the ground we stood on,
and the misty rain then falling gave me a complete
Idea of a deluge — Ailsa struck me very suddenly —
really I was a little alarmed.[13]

Alarmed by the vision, the poet finds himself looking down upon a drowned world; the vast age of the earth and the immensity of the forces that have shaped it come upon him like the huge rock itself, which is locked in its 'two dead eternities', first deep down 'with the Whales' and now high up 'with the eglle [eagle] skies'. 'When from the Sun was thy broad forehead hid?', he asks the rock, 'How long ist since the mighty Power bid / Thee heave to airy sleep from fathom dreams' — imagery which unmistakably finds its way into Book II (ll. 10-12) of *Hyperion*:

> Crag jutting forth to crag, and rocks that seemed
> Ever as if just rising from a sleep,
> Forehead to forehead held their monstrous horns

Another island appears across another sea in Bashō's *Oku no hosomichi*. The island is Sado, off the Japan Sea coast of modern Niigata Prefecture:

> 荒海や佐渡によこたふ天河
>
> *araumi ya*
> *Sado ni yokotau*
> *ama no gawa*
>
> Over a tossing sea
> the Milky Way
> arches to Sado.

---

[13] Letter to Tom Keats of 10-14 July 1818; Gittings, pp. 125-26. Had Keats read *The Prelude* when he wrote this? His alarm at the sight of Ailsa Craig immediately recalls Wordsworth's boyhood prank of taking a boat without permission out on Ullswater and *his* alarm at seeing a 'huge Cliff' rear up and stride after him as he rows away from the shore. I refer to Book I, ll. 372-427 in the 1805 text of *The Prelude* edited by Ernest de Selincourt and corrected by Stephen Gill (Oxford: Oxford University Press, 1970).

Bashō tells us[14] that at the time he wrote this *haiku* he was suffering from exhaustion and a bout of a recurring illness, perhaps represented by the rough sea; but what we are left with is the calm eternity of the Milky Way that connects all things in one great curve. In other words, Sado evokes a vision of peace and solace which passes transparently through any personal emotion that Bashō might feel, whereas Keats confesses himself disturbed by Ailsa Craig and it is that personal response which sets him describing the scene to Tom. The sensibilities of Keats and Bashō, it would seem, are not the same at all. However, what the poets have in common — and it is in this sense that I would say their sensibilities *are* alike — is an openness to the natural world and a capacity to express, in their own ways, the presence of something greater than themselves, and greater than ourselves.

In a melancholy scene at the end of *Oku no hosomichi*,[15] the sea itself has calmed into gentler waves that tumble together little coloured shells and fragments of wild shrub, the detritus of our ephemeral world:

浪の間や小貝にまじる萩の塵

nami no ma ya
kogai ni majiru
hagi no chiri

Mingled in the waves —
small shells and
tatters of bush clover.

Earlier, in a prose passage as beautifully balanced as a *haiku*, a fabled pine tree speaks for a state of natural harmony that will always return to itself, no matter how wilfully or thoughtlessly man may disturb it, and no matter how long it takes:

My heart leaped with joy when I saw the celebrated
pine tree of Takekuma, its twin trunks shaped exactly

---

[14] Yuasa, pp. 130-31. As a personal interpretation for which I have no objective evidence to hand, Sado may have symbolic significance for Bashō. The island was known for its gold and silver mines (an important source of revenue to the Tokugawa regime) but also as a place of exile: the first person believed to have been banished there, in the year 722, was a poet.

[15] Yuasa, p. 141.

17

as described by the ancient poets. I was immediately reminded of the Priest Nōin, who had grieved to find upon his second visit this same tree cut [down] and thrown into the River Natori as bridge-piles by the newly-appointed governor of the province. This tree had been planted, cut, and replanted several times in the past, but just when I came to see it myself it was in its original shape after a lapse of perhaps a thousand years, the most beautiful shape one could possibly think of for a pine tree.[16]

At the earthy end of the scale, Keats and Bashō had no choice but to be open to the hardships and indignities of travel in remote regions. Keats grumbles about dirty lodgings, bad food, and the unwanted companionship of 'cursed Gad flies', which, he is convinced, have been 'at' him ever since he left London.[17] On the whole, though, Keats appears to have been less taken with the creative possibilities of personal discomfort than Bashō, who, after one particularly miserable night in a gatekeeper's hut in the mountains,[18] pens the following *haiku*:

蚤虱馬の尿する枕もと

nomi shirami
uma no bari suru
makura moto

Fleas and lice,
horses pissing nearby —
such was my sleeping place.

It may be that it was through such experiences in their own lives that Keats and Bashō were open to the experiences of destitute and semi-outcast people at the margins of society, whose very existence would have been unknown or of no interest in London or Edo. One of the most remarkable descriptions in all of Keats's letters — all the more remarkable for its misleading tone — occurs in the account of his brief

---

[16] Yuasa, p. 111.

[17] Letter to Tom Keats of 17-21 July 1818; Gittings, p. 130.

[18] Yuasa, p. 120.

and abortive detour to Ireland. Returning to the port of Donaghadee after abandoning his planned visit to the Giant's Causeway in Antrim, Keats encounters 'the Duchess of Dunghill', an old woman puffing on a pipe as she is carried along on a sort of improvised palanquin by two equally ragged girls. The scene is outlandish, grotesque, the old woman portrayed as barely human ('squat like an ape [...] looking out with a round-eyed skinny lidded, inanity'), and yet Keats cannot help asking himself, '*What a thing would be a history of her Life and sensations*'.[19] There is a tension here, it seems to me, between Keats's undisguised revulsion at what he has witnessed and the impulse to wonder, almost in spite of himself, what it would be like to live a life of such wretchedness. The closest equivalent to the 'Duchess of Dunghill' incident in *Oku no hosomichi* is Bashō's overnight stay at Ichiburi, the provincial border post where he has arrived exhausted and in poor health.[20] He is kept awake by the sound of whispering voices in a nearby room: two prostitutes from Niigata, on their way to worship at the great shrine in Ise about two hundred miles to the south, are talking with an old man who has accompanied them as far as Ichiburi but who is turning back the next day. Bashō is deeply moved as they entrust the old man with messages they have written for their friends in Niigata. Probably indentured to their brothel for years to come, the women are trapped in a world of calculated deceit, feigning love to gratify one client after another; what offence must they have committed in an earlier life, they lament, to be destined now to wash ashore like the foam left by breakers. Missing from Bashō's description of the prostitutes, we notice, is the tone of disgust in Keats's description of the old woman in Ireland. Bashō is, as we would say, completely non-judgemental: the only thing he feels towards the two women is compassion — a Buddhist virtue, yes, but also his natural and unambivalent inclination.

All of this raises one last question: how did Keats and Bashō themselves explain their reasons for taking to the road? In Keats's case, it is tempting to turn once more to his letter to Reynolds of 19 February 1818 and the wonderful reflections there on the 'fine Webb' and 'tapestry empyrean' of man's soul, 'full of Symbols for his spiritual eye, of softness for his spiritual touch, of space for his wandering'. Although the 'Minds of Mortals are so different and bent on such

[19] Letter to Tom Keats of 3-9 July 1818; Gittings, p. 120. My italics.

[20] Yuasa, pp. 131-32.

diverse Journeys', Keats says, it is a mistake to think that there can be no 'common taste and fellowship' between them. Quite the reverse:

> Minds would leave each other in contrary directions, traverse each other in Numberless points, and all [at] last greet each other at the Journeys end — A old Man and a child would talk together and the old Man be led on his Path, and the child left thinking — Man should not dispute or assert but whisper results to his neighbour, and thus by every germ of Spirit sucking the Sap from mould ethereal every human might become great, and Humanity instead of being a wide heath of Furse and Briars with here and there a remote Oak or Pine, would become a grand democracy of Forest Trees.[21]

Our wanderings, however diverse and contrary, lead us back to our shared humanity, and it is by greeting each other again at journey's end and whispering our results that we can hope for the grand democracy of Forest Trees. This would have been a fine manifesto for Keats's journey to northern England and Scotland, but it is far removed from what he actually said when, less than two months later, he told Benjamin Haydon of the forthcoming trip:

> I purpose within a Month to put my knapsack at my back and make a pedestrian tour through the North of England, and part of Scotland — to make a sort of Prologue to the Life I intend to pursue — that is to write, to study and to see all Europe at the lowest expence. I will clamber through the Clouds and exist.[22]

On the one hand, Keats's declared intention of making his tour into 'a sort of Prologue' to his life is endearingly earnest. As he tells Benjamin Bailey from Inveraray,[23] he would not be 'tramping in the highlands' if he did not think that it would 'give me more experience, rub off more

[21] Gittings, p. 66.

[22] Letter to Haydon dated 8 April 1818; Gittings, p. 83.

[23] Letter to Bailey of 18, 22 July 1818; Gittings, p. 137.

Prejudice, use [me] to more hardship, identify finer scenes load me with grander Mountains, and strengthen more my reach in Poetry' than staying at home with his books. Directly or indirectly, Keats was indeed rewarded for his pains with some of the aphoristic insights for which we most admire him, including 'Nothing ever becomes real till it is experienced — Even a Proverb is no proverb to you till your Life has illustrated it'.[24] On the other hand, the letter to Haydon is strangely contradictory, a little disappointing even. Keats had criticized Wordsworth for poetry that 'has a palpable design upon us' and yet, it strikes me, there is something of a palpable design *upon himself,* a too-eager, conscious purposiveness in Keats's own motivation for the trip to Scotland. What I am trying to suggest may be clearer if we set Keats's letter against the opening lines of *Oku no hosomichi*:

> Days and months are travellers of eternity. So are the
> years that pass by. Those who steer a boat across the
> sea, or drive a horse over the earth till they succumb
> to the weight of years, spend every minute of their
> lives travelling. There are a great number of ancients,
> too, who died on the road. I myself have been
> tempted for a long time by the cloud-moving wind —
> filled with a strong desire to wander.[25]

The clue, as they say, is in the title. The *Oku* of *Oku no hosomichi* comes from the Japanese reading of a Chinese character (奥) meaning 'interior' or 'the innermost part', which here denotes not just the wild northern provinces of feudal Japan but also a sense close to that of the English word 'soul'. Bashō's journey through the interior of Japan is a journey through the soul, but there is nothing designed, nothing too eager, nothing consciously purposive in the way he goes about it. He is filled with a strong desire to wander. It is of no concern to him whether or not he returns. There is nothing more to be said.

The comparison with Bashō is unfair, of course. Again in his own disarmingly ingenuous words,[26] Keats was 'not old enough or magnanimous enough to anihilate self', while Bashō, established

---

[24] Letter to George and Georgiana Keats of 14 February-3 May 1819; Gittings, p. 230.

[25] Yuasa, p. 97.

[26] Letter to Bailey of 10 June 1818; Gittings, p. 99.

master of his own school of poetry, was beyond the edgy sensitivities and drive for personal recognition that he, like Keats, may have felt as a young man. Above all, Bashō was steeped in a centuries-old, Buddhist-influenced literary tradition that returned again and again to the transitoriness of this world and the vanity of all our individual cares and ambitions.[27] Unfair as the comparison is, perhaps we have to say that Bashō was the better traveller because, so to speak, he was better equipped to annihilate self. Conversely, perhaps we can also allow ourselves to believe that, had Keats lived to Bashō's age, he would have travelled many narrow roads of his own throughout the British Isles and continental Europe. And if he had, what a thing would have been the history of that life and those sensations?

Acknowledgement

I wish to thank Professor Nobuyuki Yuasa for kindly allowing me to quote from his prose translations in *The Narrow Road to the Deep North and Other Travel Sketches*, first published in 1966.

---

[27] Among prose works I am thinking, for example, of the *Hōjōki* (*An Account of My Hut*) by Kamo no Chōmei, a former court poet turned Buddhist priest and recluse, which begins 'The flow of the river is ceaseless and its water is never the same.' Written four years before his death in 1216, it is a haunting meditation on the natural disasters and other calamities he has witnessed. There is a translation by Donald Keene in the *Anthology of Japanese Literature to the Mid-Nineteenth Century* (various editions, including a Penguin Classics in 1968).

Bashō's Frog, the Great Survivor

In this essay I use the historically more correct term hokku *rather than the familiar* haiku: *for most purposes they denote the same thing, a 17-syllable poem usually in the order 5-7-5. The word* haikai, *which occurs on pages 24 and 25, I use in its broadest sense to encompass several related genres, including* hokku, haiku, *and* haibun *(mixed prose/poetry).*

古池や蛙飛こむ水の音

furuike ya
kawazu tobikomu
mizu no oto

The old pond —
a frog jumps in,
the sound of water.

Let's just call it the 'What's all the fuss about?' school of thought. That is, there are those who think Bashō's frog hokku has been the subject of too much oversubtle interpretation — mystification, in fact — and accorded an importance it does not deserve. The scholar Naitō Meisetsu, for example, writing in 1904, put it as follows:

> There was an old pond, a frog jumped into it, and — plop! — the sound of water was heard. That is all the poem says. The interest of the poem lies in its being purely descriptive of the scene. It goes without saying that this hokku does not rank high among Bashō's poems. I am certain Bashō and his disciples did not expect future readers to value [it] so highly or to attach so many surprising meanings to it.[1]

---

[1] Translation by Makoto Ueda, in his *Bashō and His Interpreters* (Stanford: Stanford University Press, 1992), p. 141. Copyright 1992 by the Board of Trustees of the Leland Stanford Junior University.

This is a minority view, of course, and the consensus now is that Bashō's frog fully deserves the importance attached to it because it marks a dividing point, a pre-amphibian/post-amphibian moment, as it were, not just in the development of Bashō's poetry but in the broader haikai tradition as well. Ironically, the roots of the modern consensus largely go back to a series of articles, *Bashō zatsudan* (*Small Talk about Bashō,* published in 1893-94), in which the poet and critic Masaoka Shiki set out, in effect, to debunk Bashō and his school. The idolatry that had built up around Bashō had to be stripped away, said Shiki, so that there could be a more genuinely critical reappraisal and appreciation of his poetry. The frog hokku was a good candidate for reappraisal because, for Shiki, its spare descriptiveness — Meisetsu's 'That is all the poem says' — was not a limitation or weakness but something new and unique:

> This poem is nothing more than a report of what the poet's auditory nerves sensed. Not only did it include none of his subjective ideas or visual, moving images, but what it recorded was nothing more than a moment of time. For that reason, this poem has no breadth in time or space. That is why no poem can be simpler than this; it is why this poem is impossible to imitate.[2]

In a later essay devoted specifically to the poem, Shiki was clear that it is not Bashō's *best* hokku (and equally clear that Bashō and his disciples did not think it his best, either). That was not the point. The significance of the hokku, said Shiki, is that it represents Bashō's realization that he had been mistaken in supposing only thoughts of dying alone on a gloomy journey, sorrow for an abandoned child, or other such 'extreme things' could be the stuff of poetry, and that, on the contrary, 'something ordinary can immediately become poetry.' Here the something ordinary just happened to be a frog jumping into an old pond.[3]

---

[2] Ueda translation, again from *Bashō and His Interpreters*, p. 141. All the remaining prose and poetry translations in this essay are my own.

[3] Shiki's essay, published in 1898, is translated in full as 'Shiki on Furu-ike ya' in R.H. Blyth's *A History of Haiku* (Tōkyō: Hokuseidō Press, 1969), Vol. II, pp. 46-76.

In our own day, Haruo Shirane has added another dimension to our appreciation of Bashō's frog hokku by exploring its subversive quality of 'working against' conventional poetic expectations. To explain what he means, Shirane invokes the account by Shikō, one of Bashō's disciples, of how the hokku was composed on a spring day in 1686.[4] A gentle rain was falling, says Shikō, and every so often could be heard the sound of frogs hopping into the pond in Bashō's garden. After silent reflection, Bashō came out with the last twelve syllables:

蛙飛こむ水の音
kawazu tobikomu
mizu no oto

a frog jumps in,
the sound of water.

Another disciple, Kikaku, suggested five syllables to begin the hokku:

山吹や
yamabuki ya

Golden kerria —

Bashō disregarded *yamabuki ya* and completed the hokku himself with the wording we know today:

古池や
furuike ya

The old pond —

The *yamabuki* (*Kerria japonica* to the botanist) with its bright yellow flowers was one of many associations with 'frog', itself a season word for spring, that haikai poets had inherited from classical poetry dating back to the Heian period and earlier. If Bashō had chosen *yamabuki ya* rather than *furuike ya*, Shirane argues, it 'would have left [his] hokku within the circle of classical associations. Instead Bashō worked against what was considered the "poetic essence" (*hon'i*), the

---

[4] Shikō's account comes from his *Kuzu no matsubara*: first published in 1692, it is virtually contemporaneous with the events it describes.

25

established classical associations, of the frog. In place of the plaintive voice of the frog singing in the rapids or calling out for his lover, Bashō gave the sound of the frog jumping into the water.'[5] Mind you, as Shirane himself points out, the same observation had been made not much more than eighty years after Bashō's death, and more succinctly, in a hokku by Buson:

飛こんで古歌洗う蛙かな

tobikonde
furu-uta arau
kawazu kana

Jumping in,
washing an old poem clean —
a frog.

For Buson, we feel, it was not so much a question of 'working against' as *breaking free from* the constrictions of stifling, codified convention.

Buson, Shiki, and now Shirane all help to explain why Bashō's frog is generally held in such high esteem today. Along the way, though, and quite apart from the scepticism of people like Meisetsu, the hokku has had to put up with a variety of indignities, some mild, others more grievous. At the mild end of the scale is the ink drawing by Sengai (1750-1837, head priest of the Shōfukuji, a temple of the Rinzai Zen sect in Hakata, Kyūshū) that depicts Bashō's frog crouching under a banana plant. The plant is a visual pun on Bashō's pen name, *bashō* being the Japanese for *Musa basjoo*, a variety of non-fruiting banana. Obvious enough. But above the drawing, in an imaginative leap of its own, the frog gently parodies Bashō with this mock-hokku:

池あらば飛んで芭蕉に聞かせたい

ike araba
tonde Bashō ni
kikasetai

If there were a pond,
I'd jump right in and have
Bashō hear the sound.

---

[5] Haruo Shirane, *Traces of Dreams: Landscape, Cultural Memory, and the Poetry of Bashō* (Stanford: Stanford University Press, 1998), p. 15. Reprinted with his permission.

An almost exact contemporary of Sengai was the poet and Zen priest Ryōkan (who was considered an eccentric recluse, and spent most of his life in what is now Niigata Prefecture in northern Japan). His response to Bashō's frog was as follows:

新池や蛙飛こむ音のなし

araike ya
kawazu tobikomu
oto no nashi

The new pond —
not so much as the sound of
a frog jumping in.

At first sight this, too, looks like nothing more than an affectionate parody. Yet could there also be a Zen element in Ryōkan's poem? Is it intimating that, at one and the same instant, an old pond, a frog, and the sound of water are there and not there? (More on Zen below.)

Moving towards the more serious end of the indignity scale takes us, I think, into the realms of translation. As I am only qualified to speak about translation into English, I will confine myself to that, although I appreciate that the frog hokku must have been translated into any number of other languages. While there are lots of perfectly good English translations, it has to be said that there are one or two excruciatingly bad ones. The prize for the most excruciating should probably go to the following, collected by R.H. Blyth and identified by him as 'No. VII of a Monograph Committee, Los Angeles, 1964':[6]

Old pond, ancient pool:
A frog jumping plunges in:
Waterish splash-splosh.

(Albeit an extreme case, this strikes me as a perfect illustration of tail wagging dog: by insisting on trying to replicate the 5-7-5 syllable count of the Japanese, the translators have ended up with repetitive gibberish. Except in the fortuitous instances where it does work, the 5-7-5 scheme is an unnatural — and, in my view, unnecessary — constraint in English translation. I digress.) On balance, I suspect that Bashō would

---

[6] *A History of Haiku*, Vol. II, p. 350.

have preferred Alfred Marks's limerick, which may be guilty of irreverent frivolity but not the crassness of the Monograph Committee translation:

> There once was a curious frog
> Who sat by a pond on a log
> And, to see what resulted,
> In the pond catapulted
> With a water-noise heard round the bog.[7]

Arguably the greatest indignity suffered by Bashō's frog — and whether you agree with this or not will depend on your own interpretation of the hokku — is its identification with, or some might say its hijacking by, Zen Buddhism. On the face of it, this appears to be a phenomenon associated with the Western 'discovery' of Bashō's poetry and its popularization, in the English-speaking world, at least, by Blyth and others. Certainly we are familiar with Blyth's conflation of haiku with Zen (and with aspects of Wordsworth), 'Haiku is a kind of *satori*, or enlightenment, in which we see into the life of things',[8] but is that the full picture? Is there anything comparable in the critical literature written by *Japanese* scholars and commentators? The answer is not black and white. Yes, in Japan there is a history of interpreting the frog hokku in Zen terms, and it long predates the Western 'discovery' of Bashō. Moreover, while some of these indigenous interpretations are cautious and nuanced in reading Zen content into the hokku, others do so very explicitly. To the best of my knowledge, however, no authoritative Japanese commentator has ever claimed, as Blyth does with characteristic extravagance, that 'If we say then that haiku is a form of Zen, we must not assert that haiku belongs to Zen, but that Zen belongs to haiku.'[9]

In the Japanese literature, one of the most unambiguously Zen readings of Bashō's frog appears in a commentary dated 1795. '[The

---

[7] From 'Haiku in Japanese and English', in *Chanoyu Quarterly* 9 (1972), p. 60. My thanks to the Uransenke Foundation, both for permission to reprint the limerick and for sharing their archive copy of the article. To be fair to the late Dr Marks, his intent was to illustrate how a particular poetic form or rhythm may work in one language but not in another.

[8] *Haiku* (Tōkyō: Hokuseidō Press, 1950), Vol. I Preface, p. vii.

[9] *Haiku*, Vol. I Preface, p. v.

hokku] should be taken in with one's eyes closed, seated on a straw mat,' according to Shinten-ō Nobutane, who goes on:

> In the Hōreki era [1751-1764] the Zen monk Hakuin often spoke about the sound of one hand [clapping]. Likewise, in this poem the sound of water is everything and nothing, nothing and everything.[10]

By contrast, the twentieth-century critic Yamamoto Kenkichi is more oblique in his reading. While he does not doubt that Zen played a significant role in the overall development of Bashō's mature style, Yamamoto is circumspect about the frog hokku itself. The reason why it has been interpreted in Zen terms, he suggests, is to do with the nature of Basho's poetic imagination. In common with Shirane, Yamamoto alludes to Shikō's account of how Bashō chose *furuike ya* over *yamabuki ya* for the opening phrase of the hokku. For Yamamoto, too, Bashō's choice is at the heart of the matter, and it is not, or not necessarily, a Zen matter. As he expresses it:

> The phrase *furuike* is not a 'combination' [*toriawase*] device like *yamabuki*. It is an essence, so to speak, distilled from the scene created by the next twelve syllables, and it reveals the core of Bashō's poetic understanding. Conversely, we might say that the poem is multi-layered: what is grasped immediately and intuitively in the first five syllables is grasped concretely, in more detail, and reflectively in the last twelve syllables. A 'combination' device principally works by setting up a *visual* image that connects the elements of the poem at an outer level of consciousness, but here the elements resonate with each other at a deeper and more fundamental level of consciousness. Compared with a 'combination' poem, Bashō's way of doing it works by evoking the *auditory* imagination, and comes from his more profound experience of language.[11]

---

[10] From Nobutane's *Oi no soko* (*Bottom of the Knapsack*), an eight-volume critical commentary on Bashō's hokku. Almost nothing is known about Nobutane himself.

[11] My translation is from Yamamoto's *Bashō: sono kanshō to hihyō* (Tōkyō: Shinchōsha, 1959), Vol. I, pp. 126-27.

Unlike Yamamoto, other twentieth-century Japanese commentators persisted with explicitly Zen interpretations. Among them was the philosopher Takeuchi Yoshinori, who, in an essay[12] that touches incidentally but tellingly on Bashō's hokku, speaks of its 'dynamic character'. By this Takeuchi partly means the 'interaction and interrelation' between the stillness of the old pond and the motion of the leaping frog, which he accentuates by expanding and translating the hokku as follows (typography as in Takeuchi's English-language text):

> The old pond —
> a frog jumps in;
> the water sounds —
> The old pond!

Now this stillness — sound — stillness 'dynamic', which suggests that, paradoxically, the serenity of the scene is all the greater for being interrupted momentarily, is also found in many interpretations of Bashō's hokku that make no mention at all of Zen. But Takeuchi's context is quite specific: the purpose of his essay is to discuss, approvingly, 'pure experience' and later developments in the philosophy of Nishida Kitarō (which, very roughly speaking, seeks to express Zen insights through some of the concepts and language of Western philosophy), and it is clear that Takeuchi's own understanding of Bashō's 'dynamic' is heavily influenced by Zen.

Perhaps the most striking Zen interpretation of Bashō's frog by a Japanese commentator (and surely one that would have made a great impression on Blyth) is offered by D.T. Suzuki in his book *Zen and Japanese Culture*, originally published in English in 1938.[13] Suzuki begins with an alternative account of the composition of the hokku. While he agrees that it came into being back-to-front, with the first five syllables added after the rest, he suggests it was under very different circumstances. It is known that in the early 1680s Bashō practised meditation under the guidance of a Zen master named Bucchō. One

---

[12] 'The Philosophy of Nishida', which originally appeared in the journal *Japanese Religions* in 1963. Takeuchi's essay is reproduced in full in Frederick Franck, ed., *The Buddha Eye: An Anthology of the Kyoto School and Its Contemporaries* (Bloomington, Indiana: World Wisdom, Inc., 2004), pp. 183-208.

[13] Daisetz T. Suzuki, *Zen and Japanese Culture* (Princeton: Princeton University Press, 2010), pp. 239-41.

day, Suzuki says, Bucchō visited Bashō and asked, 'How are you getting on these days?', to which Bashō replied, 'After the recent rain the moss has grown greener than ever.' Bucchō then asked, 'What Buddhism is there even before the moss has grown greener?' And it was in response to this, according to Suzuki, that Bashō came out with the twelve syllables,

蛙飛こむ水の音
kawazu tobikomu
mizu no oto

a frog jumps in,
the sound of water.

The exchanges between Bucchō and Bashō are in the nature of *mondō* or *kōan*, paradoxical and seemingly meaningless utterances (including Hakuin's 'What is the sound of one hand?', alluded to by Nobutane) that are typical of Zen. We are puzzled, and even more puzzled when Suzuki refers to St John's Gospel. Bucchō's second question, Suzuki continues, is equivalent in significance to 'Before Abraham was, I am', Christ's rebuke to the Jews in the temple who accused him of insulting their patriarch.[14] In other words, implicitly both Bucchō and Christ are addressing the same question: what was there — or, as Suzuki is careful to say, what *is* there — before man, before nature, and before the world itself? Christ answers by identifying himself with God and asserting that *God is* and has always been, that is, by an appeal to Christian faith. But Bucchō's way of putting the question demands a more rigorous answer because Buddhism does not make a distinction between creation and creator, or split man and nature from some separate being above and beyond the world. Hence what Bucchō is asking is, 'Where is God even before he uttered, "Let there be light"?', which is to say, 'What is there before the world, *and before any God to create the world*?' The Zen answer is that there is time without time, space without space, an undifferentiated nothingness that nonetheless contains the possibility of everything that is and might ever be. Which brings Suzuki back to Bashō's frog and the sound it makes as it leaps into the old pond.

---

[14] John 8:58.

31

It is a mistake, Suzuki says, to understand Zen as a 'gospel of quietism', and it is a mistake to understand Bashō's hokku as an 'appreciation of tranquillity'. Bashō's insight, Suzuki insists, is not into the silence of still water in a shady garden, but into the sound of water as the silence is broken. The frog, the pond, the poet, the whole universe itself, are all dissolved in that one sound and united in the undifferentiated nothingness. 'Bashō's old pond,' Suzuki concludes, 'lies on the other side of eternity, where timeless time is. [...] It is whence all things come, it is the source of this world of particulars, yet in itself it shows no particularization. We come to it when we go beyond the "rainfall" and "the moss growing greener".'

On one level, it is difficult to know what to make of Suzuki's interpretation. Although he does not identify it as such, his alternative account of the frog hokku's composition actually comes from *A True History of Master Bashō's 'Old Pond'*,[15] published in 1868 by the poet Kitsuda Shunko, which Yamamoto describes as 'nonsense' and others regard as a hoax. But maybe authenticity of source is not the issue here. Whether as an elaborate metaphor, imaginative licence, or however else Suzuki might mean us to take the *True History* account itself, his own commentary on it represents one of the profoundest of the Zen interpretations of Bashō's hokku and, in my opinion, is the one that rings the truest.

*****

What is the moral of the story? How do we account for the fact that after more than three hundred years Bashō's frog hokku keeps drawing us back, and, chances are, will still be drawing readers back in another three hundred years? How come everything that could possibly be said about its seventeen syllables has not been said long ago, definitively, once and for all? Particularly as Shiki and Yamamoto have both picked up on the auditory element — the sound of water — in the hokku, an auditory, or even a musical, analogy seems apt. In a rare interview in 1998, the Estonian composer Arvo Pärt was asked, indirectly, what he was trying to say in his music and what he thought his audiences expected when they came to hear it. Pärt's answer, equally indirect, was: 'Perhaps together with the audience, we [composer, orchestra, choir and conductor] are at the same distance from something larger.' For Pärt, a devout Russian Orthodox Christian, the 'something larger'

---

[15] *Bashō-ō furuike shinden*, purportedly transcribed from a rediscovered manuscript.

32

in music may well be God, but he does not assume that anyone else will perceive it in the same way. 'There are as many different ways of perception as there are listeners,' he adds, 'and all of them are justified.'[16] Is the secret of the longevity of Bashō's hokku, then, precisely that it *cannot* be pinned down and interpreted definitively, once and for all? If there is something larger in it, and most of us feel that there is, it is something that no one can agree on. Whether we put our own interpretations on the poem, or accept it as an unadorned report of Bashō's faculty of hearing, a casting-off of tired convention, a moment of Zen insight, or, indeed, a case of 'What's all the fuss about?', in Pärt's sense every one of our responses is justified.

---

[16] Pärt's interview appeared in the Estonian-language newspaper *Postimees* on 12 June 1998. The translation is by Alan Teder, reproduced with his permission.

Found in Translation

No. Let's start again.... What does Bashō say just before the haiku?

> In the domain of Yamagata there is a mountain temple
> called the Ryūshakuji. Founded by the revered priest
> Jikaku, the temple is a place of pure tranquillity.
> Everyone keeps saying we should see it, so we double
> back there from Obanazawa, a detour of about
> seventeen miles. It is still light when we arrive. We
> arrange lodgings at the foot of the mountain, then
> climb to the shrines near the summit. The mountain is
> made of massive rocks piled one on top of another,
> covered with ancient pines and oaks. Earth and stone
> are time-worn and smooth with moss. The shrines
> perched on the rocks all have their doors shut. Not a
> sound. We work our way round the sheer cliffs,
> crawling on hands and knees from rock to rock and
> worshipping at each shrine. In the hushed beauty of
> these surroundings, the heart knows nothing but peace.

Pretty straightforward until we get to 'the heart knows nothing but peace', *kokoro sumiyuku nomi oboyu*. Key word is *sumiyuku*, 'becomes transparent': here describes a state of mind — or 'heart', the literal meaning of *kokoro*, which works fine in English — that is now crystal clear, like turbid water after sediment has dissolved away. In its inner state, the heart exactly mirrors the 'pure tranquillity' of the external surroundings.

How do other translators do it?

At one extreme, Nobuyuki Yuasa spells it out very fully with 'I felt the purifying power of this holy environment pervading my whole being.' At the other extreme is Sam Hamill, who pares Bashō's prose right down to 'I sat, feeling my heart begin to open.' 'I sat' is poetic licence as Bashō doesn't say whether he is sitting or standing at this point, yet it's imaginatively justified, and 'feeling my heart begin to open' is simple and direct. And directness is what matters, the experience before any attempt at understanding or explanation....

What about going all the way to 'the heart knows nothing but *itself*' — the heart so transparent, the sediment so completely dissolved, that nothing clouds it, not even awareness of the surroundings?

Problem: 'the heart ... itself' might be misunderstood as making 'heart' synonymous with 'consciousness', or with 'self' in the familiar sense of our awareness of 'I-ness' or 'me-ness'. And that would look like an act of cultural hijacking because, whatever else Bashō may mean by *kokoro sumiyuku*, it has nothing to do with an inward-looking consciousness or the 'I/me' self — on the contrary, surely he's suggesting a suspension or negation of the 'I/me' self. Keep it simple and stick with 'knows nothing but peace'.

Why 'the heart' and not 'my heart'?

No help from Bashō, who doesn't use personal pronouns or their determiners, but it's true 'my' is the obvious choice. Trouble is English demands pronouns, and we've already committed — you agreed — to 'we' to recognize that Bashō has climbed to the summit together with his companion, Sora: 'our hearts know nothing but peace' would be presumptuous (Sora might be feeling something completely different for all anyone knows!), while switching to 'my heart' is both awkward and avoidable since 'the heart' is equally natural in this context. QED.

All right.... We've come full circle, back to the haiku:

> *shizukasa ya*
> *iwa ni shimiiru*
> *semi no koe*

Back to the haiku, and back to our three complications. Firstly, the translation of *shizukasa* ('stillness', 'quiet') should also evoke something akin to *sabishisa* (with the nuance 'serene solitude' rather than the dictionary definition, 'loneliness') because, instead of writing *shizukasa* with the Chinese character normally used for that word, Bashō has chosen a different character that visually conveys a sense of *sabishisa*. In Japanese it works almost as a form of synaesthesia — the ear hears *shizukasa*, so to speak, while the eye sees *sabishisa* — but can the effect be approximated somehow in English? Second complication: *shimiiru* has a spectrum of possible translations, ranging from 'permeate' or 'seep in' at the softer end through to 'pierce' or 'bite in' at the stronger end. Which to go for? And thirdly, Japanese does not distinguish between singular and plural: are you going to translate *iwa ni* as 'into a rock' or 'into the rocks', and *semi no koe* as 'a cicada's voice' or 'cicadas' voices'?

Start with the singular/plural conundrum.... How about making *iwa* 'the rock' and then it's as ambiguous as the Japanese: could be a single rock — 'that big one over there' — or many rocks treated as a sort of collective noun — 'the rock of the whole mountain, made up of individual rocks piled on top of each other'.

Done, 'into the rock'. Have to make an explicit choice, though, with *semi*.

'Cicadas' plural is more plausible because it's unlikely there would only be one cicada among all those trees on the mountain. On the other hand, a single cicada is quite capable of making its presence known by its repertoire of distinctive sounds, some of which are ear-splitting in volume and pitch. The decider: where 'cicadas' anticipates a rolling, repeating cacophony extended over time, 'cicada' anticipates sound focused into a single moment, which is better suited to the arrested-in-time feel of a haiku. One cicada it is.

Next the *shizukasa/sabishisa* question. Some translators seem to ignore it altogether. Hamill has 'Lonely stillness' — 'stillness' for *shizukasa* and 'lonely' for *sabishisa*. Yuasa opts for 'utter silence' — 'silence' for *shizukasa* and 'utter' perhaps for *sabishisa*. Any improvement on their attempts?

Yes, maybe, although it involves a bit of lateral thinking. Or cheating, depending on how you look at it. In the course of their 1,500-mile journey around northern Japan, Sora recorded almost all the haiku composed by Bashō, himself, and others, and his record reveals that in Bashō's first version of this haiku the first four syllables were not *shizukasa* but *yamadera*, 'mountain temple'. Now 'mountain temple' immediately recalls the images of the Ryūshakuji and its precincts that Bashō has conjured up in his prose description, especially the early-evening atmosphere, the shrines with their doors closed, and the unbroken silence. These are all images of deep solitude and serenity — just the qualities of *sabishisa* suggested by the Chinese character Bashō has chosen to use. If we take the 'mountain' of 'mountain temple' for what the eye sees in Japanese, *sabishisa*, 'stillness' for the what the ear hears, *shizukasa*, the first line of the translation becomes 'Mountain stillness'. May be as close as we can get to the the semi-synaesthetic effect Bashō achieves. More or less happy with it?

Yes ... provided you don't forget Bashō's fifth syllable, *ya*, the *kireji* or 'cutting word'.

36

As its function is to indicate a pause, somewhere between a comma and a full stop in duration, closest equivalent in English is probably a dash. Agree with 'Mountain stillness —'?

Agree.

That leaves *shimiiru*. Let's not beat about the bush. Or the tree. The back-to-front subject of the verb, the thing that's doing the *shimiiru*, is *semi no koe*, 'a cicada's voice'. There's our clue: a cicada doesn't have a 'voice', and nor does it 'cry', 'trill', or 'sing', as some translators would have it. There are species of cicadas that *screech*, *shriek*, or *shrill*, make harsh and unnerving sounds that, fortuitously, are sibilant in English — 'a cicada's shrieking', 'a cicada's shrilling' — and complement the assonance of Bashō's *i-wa ni shi-mi-i-ru se-mi* (which in turn perhaps mimics the sound of one or other species?). But it's not the main point, which is that 'screech', 'shriek' and 'shrill' do not, or not obviously, invite softer translations of *shimiiru* such as 'seep in' or 'sink in'. Some trial and error required.

OK, trial and error. Put it all together, try first with 'sink in' and see what happens:

> Mountain stillness —
> a cicada's shrilling
> sinks into the rock

Hmm. Apart maybe from 'mountain' for *sabishisa*, it's faithful to the Japanese, uncontroversial, safe.... Too safe? Translated this way, what is Bashō saying?

Perfect stillness is broken by the shrilling of a cicada. The shrilling sinks into the rock, and stillness returns. Paradoxically, the stillness is all the greater for the sudden breaking of it.

Difficult to object to that interpretation, yet still can't help feeling it's non-committal. What if Bashō means that the shrilling is lost not just in the rock, but in the stillness itself? The stillness is so profound that it cancels out or, a very free translation of *shimiiru*, 'swallows up' the shrilling?

> Mountain stillness —
> a cicada's shrilling
> is swallowed up in the rock

Or what if he means the exact opposite — it's not the stillness that prevails, but the raucous sound of the cicada? In that case, definitely need to go to the more forceful end of the *shimiiru* spectrum:

> Mountain stillness —
> a cicada's shrilling
> penetrates the rock

Is there a paradox after all? There was stillness, then a loud noise, and now either the noise is gone or the stillness is gone....

Yes, I see what you're trying to do.

Eh?

One way or another, you're trying to tidy up or explain away the paradox.

Well, why not? It's not some uniquely Western intolerance of contradiction, if that's what you're implying. Lots of Japanese readers also find this haiku perplexing and feel that a screeching insect makes a nonsense of perfect quiet.

Not necessarily an East-West thing, no.... Hear this out. Think word order. Even to arrive at the most conservative translation, 'a cicada's shrilling / sinks into the rock', we've had to reverse Bashō's middle seven and last five syllables, *iwa ni shimiiru semi no koe*. If the priority is to be true to the Japanese *and* produce meaningful English, and it is the priority, there can't be anything sacrosanct about Bashō's word order — and that includes the placing of his first five syllables, *shizukasa ya*. So, take a deep breath, move our translation of *shizukasa ya* from the beginning to the *end* and ... far from evading or resolving the paradox, we confront it head-on. Go further. Make the paradox completely inescapable, amplifying the noise of the cicada still more by changing 'penetrates the rock' to 'pierces the rock', and deepening the quiet of the Ryūshakuji still more by changing 'mountain stillness' to ... to ... 'unbroken silence':

> A cicada's shrilling
> pierces the rock —
> unbroken silence

Translated *that* way, what is Bashō saying?

The stillness of a mountaintop temple and the shrieking of a cicada are not contradictory or mutually exclusive. Beyond — or within — what we perceive as paradox, they are two aspects of one and the same reality. Bashō's *semi no koe* stands for the reality of the ephemeral, particular world of cicadas, rocks and trees, poets, and ourselves. But it's a world that comes out of the timeless, undifferentiated reality represented by *shizukasa ya* — the *śūnyatā* of Mahāyāna Buddhism, seemingly an absolute emptiness that yet contains the possibility of every thing and every being that is and might be. The reality of the world is self-evident, insistent, all too present. To know reality in its timeless, undifferentiated aspect, the heart itself must be empty, unclouded, *kokoro sumiyuku*.

*****

I must be getting old. Why else would I find myself constantly going back over the past.

Have the courage of your convictions, boy!

In his irritable, soldierly way, Colonel Toker had tried to be encouraging as I dithered over my answer to a question in his algebra class. Nevertheless his words live on as a reproach for something in my response that was wanting then and, all these years later, seems to remain wanting. A relation to the world lived at the softer end of the spectrum, more seeping and sinking in than piercing and biting in. Non-committal. No wonder I've always been drawn to ambiguities. Small, manageable ambiguities. Contradictions nicely balanced out: on the one hand this, on the other hand that. Big, unmanageable ambiguities — inescapable conflicts — evaded altogether: anything but confront them head-on, which would mean making an explicit choice. Which would mean committing. *Non-committal.*

And now this new voice in my head:

>*shizukasa ya*
>*iwa ni shimiiru*
>*semi no koe*

>A cicada's shrilling
>pierces the rock —
>unbroken silence

What to make of it? Do I believe in my own translation? Is it wishful thinking? Am I misrepresenting Bashō? I've turned his haiku into a baffling question-and-answer exchange that, in the manner of a Zen *kōan*, confounds the rational mind and, by confounding, hopes to jolt it into a spontaneous understanding of some truth. The truth here is, for want of a better word, the *interchangeability* of everything and nothing:

> *Question: What is the sound of absolute emptiness?*
> *Answer: The screeching of a cicada.*

Is the *kōan* in the haiku or have I put it there myself? Whether or not *shizukasa ya* does represent *śūnyatā*, Bashō's image of the heart becoming clear — an image of the 'I/me' sense of self suspended or negated in a moment of profound insight — itself suggests a Buddhist element in the haiku. Specifically a Zen element? Am I unduly influenced by knowing that from about 1680, when Bashō was in his late thirties, he briefly studied meditation under a Zen priest, Bucchō, and therefore may have had direct experience of *kōan*–like exchanges? It's not much to go on. What if I've fabricated the *kōan*...?

Enough. Enough. Even if I have fabricated it, even if there is nothing in Bashō's haiku to baffle the rational understanding, there's plenty to baffle us in what we know of reality. We know, as Bashō could not have known, that the universe — and with it the possibility of our world and everything else that is and might ever be — literally came out of a great emptiness, a primordial nothingness, 13.8 billion years ago. So another truth, literal, metaphoric, or however we wish to take it, is that there are as many ways of being in the world as there are possibilities in nothingness and, in a sense, they are all valid. We are where we are, as the saying goes, and we are what we are. And this has been and is where I am and what I am, a quietly overwrought schoolboy who struggled to be fully part of his world and grew up wondering whether he wanted to be part of it at all. Is that defeatism? Weakness? Complacency? Laziness? Convention judges us. Other people judge us. We judge ourselves. Yet what judging is there — who or what is to say that one way of being is right and another wrong — in the great nothingness from which we all come?

It's been a long time in the making, Colonel Toker, but here's my answer:

If a is zero, b is an indeterminate value. That's just how it is. QED.

The Frog and the Basilisk

The Judaeo-Christian creation myth has a lot to answer for even in our supposedly secular age. In and after the European Enlightenment, the deity who had made heaven and earth became the prototype of impersonal forces — notably Universal Reason, Progress, and History — then believed to be at work in the world. These apparent secularizations of the Word of God, each of which failed in its own way, were expressions of a collective fear of the unintelligible, that is, of the very idea that the world might *just be* without reason or purpose. What follows is an attempt to explore the forms and origins of this fear, which perhaps remains unresolved in our culture to this day. It begins outside the Judaeo-Christian tradition with the world view implied, on one interpretation, in a famous *haiku* by the seventeenth-century Japanese poet Bashō. The essay ends by suggesting that secular society will achieve a completely honest accommodation with the world only when it comes to terms with the reality of the creation, namely that there was no reason, necessity, or purpose in the Big Bang that brought matter and energy into existence 13.8 billion years ago — a reality strangely prefigured in Bashō's *haiku*.

Bashō's frog

Of all Bashō's *haiku*, probably the best known — both in its original language and in translation — is about a frog:

> 古池や蛙飛こむ水のおと
> *furuike ya*
> *kawazu tobikomu*
> *mizu no oto*

This translates literally (and with arbitrary punctuation) as:

The old pond.
A frog jumps in.
The sound of water.

It dates from 1686, when Bashō, aged forty-two, was living on the outskirts of Edo, Japan's new capital, in a house near the River Sumida. According to one of his disciples, Shikō,[1] the *haiku* was composed on a fine spring day; a gentle rain was falling and every so often came the sound of frogs hopping into the pond in Bashō's garden. After a period of silent reflection, Bashō came out with the last twelve syllables:

蛙飛こむ水のおと
kawazu tobikomu
mizu no oto

Another disciple, Kikaku, suggested five syllables to begin the *haiku*:

山吹や
yamabuki ya

The golden flowers of a kerria.

Bashō considered this but then completed the *haiku* himself with the wording as we know it today:

古池や
furuike ya

The old pond.

Shikō observes that their master's wording, more 'honest' in its simplicity, could only have been chosen by one who saw into the inner truth of things: a worthy sentiment, but not one that sheds much light on the precise nature of Bashō's insight. However, an alternative account of how the frog *haiku* came to be composed was offered in 1938 by Suzuki Daisetsu (Daisetz or D.T. Suzuki as he is known in the English-speaking world), the distinguished scholar of Buddhism, in a

---

[1] The disciple's full name is Kagami Shikō. The source is 'Kuzu no matsubara' in his collected works, *Shikō zenshū* (Tōkyō: Hakubunkan, 1898), pp. 1-2.

book entitled *Zen and Japanese Culture*.[2] Told so long after the event and only loosely supported by the known facts of Bashō's life, it is difficult to judge how to characterize Suzuki's account: apocryphal, an elaborate metaphor, or a challenge to our whole sense of what distinguishes 'factual' evidence from other forms of evidence? [3] Whatever the answer may be, and perhaps it is best left to individual readers to decide, Suzuki has something to say that is far more profound — some might feel far more disturbing — than Shikō's anodyne observation.

Suzuki agrees that the frog *haiku* came into being back-to-front, with the first part added after the rest, but he suggests it was under very different circumstances. It is known that from about 1680 Bashō practised meditation under the guidance of a Zen master named Bucchō. One day, Suzuki claims, Bucchō visited Bashō and asked, 'How are you getting on these days?', to which Bashō replied, 'After the recent rain the moss has grown greener than ever.' Bucchō then asked, 'What Buddhism is there even before the moss has grown greener?' And to this, according to Suzuki, Bashō replied:

蛙飛こむ水のおと
kawazu tobikomu
mizu no oto

A frog jumps in.
The sound of water.

The exchanges between Bucchō and Bashō are in the nature of *kōan*, paradoxical and apparently meaningless utterances that are central to much Zen practice. We are baffled, and still more baffled when Suzuki alludes to St John's Gospel. Bucchō's second question, Suzuki continues, is equivalent in significance ('tantamount' is his word in the

---

[2] All the quotations that follow are from the 2010 reprint (Princeton: Princeton University Press), pp. 239-42. For a translator's perspective on the difficulties of rendering the frog *haiku* into English, see N. Yuasa's 'Translating "The sound of water"' in William Radice and Barbara Reynolds, eds., *The Translator's Art: Essays in Honour of Betty Radice* (Harmondsworth: Penguin Books, 1987), pp. 231-40.

[3] When I wrote this in 2014 I did not know that Suzuki was quoting, without attribution, from *A True History of Master Bashō's 'Old Pond'*, published in 1868 by the poet Kitsuda Shunko Supposedly a rediscovered manuscript, *A True History* is now generally regarded as dubious if not fraudulent.

English-language edition) to 'Before Abraham was, I am', Christ's rebuke to the Jews in the temple who accused him of insulting the name of their tribal patriarch.[4] In other words, implicitly both Bucchō and Jesus are asking the same question: what was there — or, as Suzuki is careful to express it, what *is* there — before man, before nature, and before the world itself? Jesus answers this by identifying himself with God and asserting that *God is* and has always been, which appeals to faith and may satisfy pious Christians. But Bucchō's way of putting the question demands a more rigorous answer because in Buddhism there is no distinction to be made between creation and creator, no splitting of man and nature from some separate being above and beyond the world. Without this splitting the question becomes, as Suzuki rephrases it, 'Where is God even before he uttered, "Let there be light"?' or, as we might rephrase it, 'What is there before man, before nature, before the world, *and before any God to create the world*?' The Zen answer: time without time, space without space, an undifferentiated nothingness that yet contains the possibility of everything that might ever be. Bashō's answer? A frog plopping into a pond.

It is a great mistake, Suzuki says, to understand Zen as a 'gospel of quietism', just as it is a great mistake to understand Bashō's frog as an evocation of sublime tranquillity. Bashō's insight, Suzuki insists, is not into the silence of still water in a shady garden, but into the *breaking* of the silence. That is, the frog, the pond, the poet, the entire universe, are all dissolved in one sound and united in the primordial nothingness. 'Bashō's old pond,' Suzuki comments, 'lies on the other side of eternity, where timeless time is. [...] No scale of consciousness can measure it. It is whence all things come, it is the source of this world of particulars, yet in itself it shows no particularization. We come to it when we go beyond the "rainfall" and "the moss growing greener".'

Suzuki had already written prolifically on the origins and content of Zen doctrine, and in his essay on the frog *haiku* he confined himself, as he put it, 'to the correct interpretation of Bashō.' His interpretation invokes modes or 'layers' of consciousness, including the 'collective unconscious' and the 'Cosmic Unconscious'. On the one hand, this is intriguing: Suzuki is saying that the concept of the unconscious as it is 'generally conceived by the psychologists' is incomplete and inadequate, and his interpretation invites comparison in particular with what Carl Jung may have meant by a 'collective unconscious'. On the

---

[4] John 8:58.

other hand, there is a risk here of falling into precisely the trap that Suzuki himself warns against: turning the frog into an *idea* and therefore an object of intellectual scrutiny, when his whole point is that the *haiku* cannot be grasped intellectually but only spontaneously and intuitively. So we would do well to keep the image of the leaping frog and let go of everything else.

Donne's basilisk

To return to the Western, biblical tradition, it has to be said that the Old Testament seems reluctant to speak of what, if anything, came before the creation. 'In the beginning,' Genesis declares, 'God created the heaven and the earth.' Yes, but out of what? If out of something, what sort of something and where did *it* come from? If out of nothing, where was God in the nothing? And if he created the universe at one particular point in time, say in the darkness preceding 23 October 4004 BC (as James Ussher, Archbishop of Armagh, was to calculate in 1650), why not 24 October, or 1 April, or 13.8 billion years earlier (currently the best scientific reckoning of the actual age of the universe)? The more the complications proliferate, the more we see why the author or authors of Genesis begin at the juncture when, although 'without form, and void', at least the earth existed and God had something to work with.

Now for a devout Christian in seventeenth-century Europe, a frog would have had a quite different significance from that of Bashō's frog in seventeenth-century Japan. Take, for instance, the sermon delivered by John Donne, metaphysical poet turned Dean of St Paul's Cathedral, London, on Easter Day in 1628. His text, from St Paul's First Epistle to the Corinthians, was 'For now we see through a glass, darkly'. We cannot hope to have an unimpeded vision of God and his works, Donne preached, until 'then', the next life; but even 'now', here in this world, we have glass enough and light enough to know that God exists. The light is the light of natural reason and the glass — the mirror — is all around us in the book of creatures:

> There is not so poor a creature but may be the glass
> to see God in. The greatest flat glass that can be made
> cannot represent anything greater than it is. If every
> gnat that flies were an archangel, all that could but
> tell me that there is a God; and the poorest worm that

creeps tells me that. If I should ask the basilisk, how camest thou by those killing eyes? he would tell me, thy God made me so; and if I should ask the slow-worm, how camest thou to be without eyes? he would tell me, thy God made me so.[5]

Although Donne makes no mention of frogs, a frog, like the slow-worm and the mythical basilisk, is a creeping thing, a product of the sixth day of creation. We can be sure, therefore, that what Donne says of the slow-worm and the basilisk he would say equally of a frog: that it is evidence not only of the work of the sixth day, but also of God's nature and, above all, his purposes. The orderliness of the creation — light from darkness, dry land from the waters, a greater light to rule day and a lesser to rule night — speaks of God's wisdom. The fecundity of the creation — plants and trees, living creatures each after their kind, and man from the dust of the ground — speaks of his munificence. Moreover, God's wisdom and munificence are purposeful, not gratuitous: the living creatures, including the creeping things, are there so that man may have dominion over them, and man is there to dress and keep the Garden of Eden. Everything in creation has a purpose, God's purpose, for being as it is.

The Word and the Word recast

When we come to the New Testament we appear to be told, albeit ambiguously, that God's purposes pre-exist the creation itself: 'In the beginning was the Word,' John chooses to say, not 'was the void' or 'was nothing'. This *Word*, we understand, is identified both with Christ and with the *Logos* of Greek philosophy, denoting a principle of creative reason, or Reason with a capital 'R', believed to be at work in the universe. But when, according to John, does God's Reason begin? If the Word is his Reason, are we to understand that Reason is the something — or maybe the nothing — out of which he created the world? Or has the writ of Reason properly run only since the creation, and especially since the moment when the Word was 'made flesh',[6]

---

[5] The sermon is reproduced in full in *The Literature of Renaissance England*, edited by John Hollander and Frank Kermode (New York: Oxford University Press, 1976), pp. 558-64.

[6] John 1:14.

that is, with the incarnation of Christ? The ambiguity remains unresolved, yet either way the New Testament, too, assures us that God has a purpose for man and the world. God has a plan.

Since Donne's age the Word has been redefined many times over, and seemingly more or less secularized in the process. In the Enlightenment of eighteenth-century Europe, the crude teleological purpose of the biblical creation story transformed itself into something subtler: a Universal Reason that lay behind all reality, the laws of which could be discovered and, once discovered, would enable mankind to remake the world through the rigorous application of rationality. Freed from metaphysics, dogma, superstition, unexamined tradition, all the stifling lore of the past, man would achieve true knowledge, virtue, and happiness; and in turn he would achieve a free and just society because, as the Marquis de Condorcet wrote in 1794 (ironically, while hiding in fear of his life in revolutionary Paris), 'Nature has united the progress of enlightenment with that of liberty, virtue, and respect for the natural rights of man'.[7] In the industrializing Britain of the nineteenth century, the Word became Progress, a new and unstoppable law evidenced for all to see in the scientific and technical marvels of the age, from its feats of engineering and navigation to manufacturing and warfare. Progress was the apotheosis of the 'new philosophy' of empirical science founded by Francis Bacon, a philosophy which, as Thomas Babington Macaulay proclaimed in 1837, 'never rests, which has never attained, which is never perfect.'[8] For others, the Word had become History, the big 'H' denoting *history that had a goal*. Far from being a random succession of one damn thing after another, History was taking us somewhere, and where it was taking us would be better than where we had come from. The history of the world, said Wilhelm Friedrich Hegel, 'is a rational process, the rational and necessary evolution of the world spirit',[9] and the reasoning of this 'spirit' was directed towards perfecting the world. Things, in time, could only get better.

---

[7] From Condorcet's *Esquisse d'un tableau historique des progrès de l'esprit humain*, quoted by Isaiah Berlin in 'Two Concepts of Liberty' in his *Four Essays on Liberty* (Oxford: Oxford University Press, 1991), p. 167 note 1.

[8] From 'Lord Bacon' in *The Works of Lord Macaulay: Essays and Biographies*, Vol. II (London: Longmans Green, 1906), p. 616.

[9] From the 1830 draft of Hegel's lectures on world history, translated by H.B. Nisbet in *Lectures on the Philosophy of World History. Introduction: Reason in History* (Cambridge: Cambridge University Press, 1989), p. 29.

Despite the differences between these and other manifestations of the Word, their common denominator was a faith in some pattern of signs, some manifest tendency, some rationale, some law, whether theological, metaphysical or 'scientific' in nature, that explained why the world was as it was and why things happened as they did. It all meant something.

Failures of the Word

What and where is the Word now? We have to start by acknowledging that the Word has survived best, and perhaps has really only survived at all, in the religious sense of a divine intelligence that orders and governs the universe. To this day millions — probably billions — of believers, most obviously creationists and other fundamentalists, hold fast to the myths and metaphors of their sacred books and treat them as literal truth. For such people God's purposes have never ceased and will remain at work until the end of time. By contrast, surely no one still seriously believes in Universal Reason as an intelligence governing the world. Although the ideals and the legacy of the Enlightenment live on, in the separation of church and state, for example, or the panoply of international legal instruments for the protection of human rights, we have lost faith in the grand promise of the Enlightenment itself: that knowledge, virtue, and happiness would be achieved, and were *bound* to be achieved, through the application of rationality alone. There must be many complex reasons why we lost this faith, but one of them is that it soon emerged that even the noblest and best-intentioned of rationalities had a tendency to turn into abstract formulae, pseudo-scientific *systems*, and new dogmas every bit as rigid and stupid and cruel as the old dogmas the Enlightenment had vowed to sweep away. In Britain, for instance, the nation that had so successfully mechanized the production of things, Jeremy Bentham set out to mechanize the production of knowledge, virtue, and especially happiness: his system was the 'principle of utility', which was going to balance pleasures and pains to ensure, automatically, the greatest happiness of the greatest number of people. Bentham's utilitarianism had grown out of an earnest concern with human happiness, and yet in effect it turned its realization into an engineering problem to be solved mathematically and mechanically. Herbert Spencer's system was evolution by natural selection reconfigured, by analogy with the evolution of individual species, as a mechanism for the perfection of society as a whole: the ideal social state would be one in which 'the completely adapted man' was in perfect accord with 'the completely evolved society'. Spencer made no apology for the fact that the weakest and least adapted members of society would suffer, and would have to suffer, as humanity was 'moulded into harmony' with the necessities of the social state because, as he put it, 'bound up with the change [is] a *normal* amount of suffering, which cannot be lessened without altering the very laws of life.'[10] Spencer's words have a chillingly sinister ring, particularly perceived from this side of the twentieth century's history of eugenics and genocide.

Our faith in Progress probably had its last gasp in the 1950s, when we were led to believe that the civil use of nuclear power would produce electricity 'too cheap to meter' and usher in a new era of prosperity and ease — a wondrous new era proclaimed in exactly the language, the same slightly delirious hyperbole, that Macaulay had used more than a century earlier.[11] In the event, the economics of building, operating, and decommissioning nuclear power plants did not translate into unlimited energy on demand, and the catastrophic accidents at Three Mile Island, Chernobyl, and now Fukushima have finally killed off our uncritical trust in such technology as an inexhaustibly benign force.

History was the most pernicious of the redefinitions of the Word, because Hegel's 'world spirit' was all too easily hijacked by ideological and nationalist interests with their own programmes of 'rational and necessary evolution'. Identified as the pseudo-historical principle of dialectical materialism, History sanctioned the Soviet Union's great experiment in political, economic, and social engineering, which turned into a monstrous project of state tyranny that cost millions of lives through famine and deliberate slaughter. Identified as the destiny of an ascendant Aryan super-race, History sanctioned the West's other monstrous project of the twentieth century, Nazism, as it sought to remake the world by triumphal will, lightning-

---

[10] These quotations are from Spencer's *The Data of Ethics* (London: Williams & Norgate, 1907, pp. 237-38) and 'The Sins of the Legislators' in *The Man versus the State* (Williams & Norgate, 1884, pp. 67-68).

[11] The notorious phrase 'too cheap to meter' can probably be blamed on Lewis Strauss, Chairman of the US Atomic Energy Commission, who used it in a speech to the National Association of Science Writers (reported in *The New York Times* of 17 September 1954, 'Abundant Power from Atom Seen').

speed conquest, and industrialized mass murder. We have to be thankful that history has dropped its big 'H' and gone back to being one damn thing after another.

The fear of the unintelligible

Whether we have called it the Word of God, Universal Reason, Progress, History or other names, the mystery is that we felt compelled to believe in any such notion to begin with. It is as if one impulse behind our whole culture, at least until relatively recently, has been a horror of things *just happening* or *just being there*, a deep intolerance of the very idea that there might be no meaningful reason for the world to be as it is (or exist at all) rather than otherwise (or not at all). It is the source of our creation myths and it is a collective delusion. For John Donne the new philosophy that called all in doubt had been Copernican astronomy,[12] but for us it is the cosmology and physics that explain how the entire universe came into being: in a Big Bang, discontinuously, something out of nothing when it might just as easily, just as logically, have remained nothing. Without reason or necessity, the universe, and therefore the possibility of everything that might ever be, *just happened*. In his *Théodicée*, published in 1710, Gottfried Wilhelm Leibniz had complained that God 'would not deserve to be wholly trusted' if his will allowed itself to act by chance, for in that case it would 'scarcely be of more value for the government of the universe than a fortuitous concourse of atoms'.[13] Leibniz has been confounded, because the will of any God that created the universe must have done exactly that — allowed itself to act so arbitrarily and randomly as to be indistinguishable from the workings of chance. If God no longer deserves to be wholly trusted, nor does our own grasp of what can reasonably be defined as reality. In the 1930s Alfred Einstein, as troubled as Leibniz by the thought of a God who played dice with the universe, spoke of his certainty that 'a conviction, akin to religious feeling, of the rationality or intelligibility of the world lies

---

[12] 'And new Philosophy calls all in doubt, / The Element of fire is quite put out; / the Sun is lost, and th' earth, and no man's wit / Can well direct him where to look for it.' From Donne's *The First Anniversary: An Anatomy of the World*, ll. 205-08.

[13] From the passage translated by Arthur Lovejoy in *The Great Chain of Being: A Study of the History of an Idea* (Cambridge, Massachusetts: Harvard University Press, 1964), pp. 166-67.

behind all scientific work of a higher order.'[14] But where is the rationality, still less the intelligibility, in matter and energy that come to be in an acausal Big Bang? Einstein is confounded as well and, it seems, we have to redefine reality to allow for the fact that the most fundamental reality of all — the origin of the universe — makes no sense to us and there is no requirement or necessity that it should. The true creation story is more fantastical than any of the mythical stories, yet it is the one we must accept.

Evolution to blame, or collective bad faith?

While evolution has equipped us with many abilities, it is a great irony that an ability to tolerate the purposeless and the unmediated does not appear to be among them. We struggle with the concept of events or processes (and some still struggle with evolution, of course) that produce orderly results and yet are themselves undirected, impartial, blind. We look for an agent or agency — and if we cannot find one, we fabricate one. *Logos*, the Word, Reason, Progress, History are all names for the collective failure of our capacity for the intelligible, or the failure of our imagination.

Or *is* evolution the culprit? Could it be something in ourselves, something more wilful, akin to bad faith? Before he abandoned his own existential philosophy, Jean-Paul Sartre might have said that much of human history has been an exercise in 'the spirit of seriousness', a form of bad faith in which we regard meanings and values — or, by extension, the reasons for things — as *facts* pre-existing in the world around us.[15] We perceive meaning as flowing *to* us *from* the world, whereas in reality, according to Sartre, meaning flows *from* us *to* the world. Fundamentally, he would say, we are guilty of bad faith when we refuse to recognize that what distinguishes us from inanimate matter is our freedom, that freedom is synonymous with our consciousness, and that consciousness is always 'at a distance' from itself and everything else in the world. Where inanimate matter is 'solid', perfectly identified and united with itself, consciousness

---

[14] 'On Scientific Truth' in Einstein's *Essays in Science*, translated by Alan Harris (New York: The Wisdom Library, 1934), p. 11.

[15] The references here and following are all to *Being and Nothingness*, translated by Hazel Barnes (London: Routledge, 1993), especially pp. 39-40, 626, 78, xli-xlii [Sartre's Introduction], and 44, in that order.

consists in a lack, a *nothingness*, between who we are now and our future possibilities. We await ourselves in the future and, if we are in good faith, project ourselves towards that future by choosing between our possibilities, which demands that we endlessly choose to act, think, and feel in one way rather than another. In bad faith, which is our more characteristic condition, we evade the unremitting demands of our freedom and try to 'fill up' the nothingness by self-deceptive means, conforming to conventional beliefs and expectations, for example, and behaving in other ways that are not of our own free choosing. Sartre's diagnosis applies to the behaviours and attitudes of individuals: is it conceivable that something similar goes on in societies and cultures writ large? Perhaps. But even if so, we have no excuse for continuing to 'fill up' the nothingness of our freedom by deluding ourselves, individually or collectively, that responsibility for what happens in the world lies with agencies whose real purpose is to absolve us of *our* responsibility.

The true creation story for a secular age

In the beginning was nothing, and there was no purpose, no design, no law in it. We know that now, or we should know it. How, then, can we go on believing that purpose, design, and law are somehow built into the fabric of our world? Finally, in the twenty-first century, is it not time to renounce the last vestiges of that belief and reach a new, more honest accommodation with the world? And if we want an image for our new accommodation, let's not make it a slow-worm, a basilisk, or any other creature imagined to be the work of a supernatural being. Let it be a frog that *just is*, leaping back into the nothingness from which it, we, and all things come:

古池や蛙飛こむ水のおと
furuike ya
kawazu tobikomu
mizu no oto

The old pond —
a frog jumps in,
the sound of water

CPSIA information can be obtained
at www.ICGtesting.com
Printed in the USA
BVHW040004160721
612047BV00013B/517